DEADLY
PREDATORS

Camilla de la Bédoyère

QED Publishing

Created for QED Publishing by Tall Tree Ltd
www.talltreebooks.co.uk
Editors: Jon Richards and Rob Colson
Designer: Jonathan Vipond
Illustration pp18–19:
Mick Posen/www.the-art-agency.co.uk

First published in the UK in 2012 by
QED Publishing
A Quarto Group company
230 City Road
London EC1V 2TT

www.qed-publishing.co.uk

A catalogue record for this book is available from the
British Library.

ISBN 978 1 84835 873 7

Printed in China

Picture credits
(t=top, b=bottom, l=left, r=right, c=centre, fc=front cover,
bc=back cover)
Alamy: 1 Steve Bloom, 10-11 Wildlife GmbH, 14-15 Mark
Conlin, 15br David Fleetham, 20-21 Gerry Pearce, 24-25
Alaska Stock, 26 blickwinkel, 26-27 Amazon-images;
Corbis 4-5 ML Sinibaldi, 11 DLILLC, 12 Thomas Kitchin &
Victoria Hurst/All Canada Photos, 17t Tom Brakefield, 17b
Theo Allofs; **Dreamstime:** 28bl Yaireibovich; **FLPA:** bctl
Pete Oxford, 7tr Malcolm Schuyl, 22bl Hiroya Minakuchi/
Minden Pictures, 29br Peter Davey; **Getty:** 12-13 Robert
Postma, 16 Vivek Sinha, 24bl Daniel J Cox, 25br Altrendo
Nature; **Nature Picture Library:** 2-3 Alex Mustard, 7b
Doug Perrine, 8-9 Doug Perrine, 9t Dan Burton, 14b Alan
James, 23t Alex Hyde, 24-25 Alex Mustard, 25t David
Fleetham, 26-27 Doug Perrine, 30-31 Jeff Rotman; **NHPA:**
bctl Andre Baertschi, 5t Martin Harvey, 6-7 Joe McDonald,
9b Daniel Hueclin, 21t Woodfall/Photoshot, 22-23 Gerard
Lacz, 28-29 Nick Garbutt, 30 Jordi Bas Casasj; **NPL:** fc
Juan Carlos Munoz, 5br Inaki Relanzon, 31r Andy Rouse;
Shutterstock: bctr Bonnie Fink, bcb neelsky; **SPL:** 3,9t
Merlin Tuttle/Bat Conservation International, 8-9 Tom
McHugh, 27t Visuals Unlimited, 31l John Shaw.

Website information is correct at time of going to press.
However, the publishers cannot accept liability for any
information or links found on any Internet sites, including
third-party websites.

Words in **bold** are explained in the Glossary on page 32.

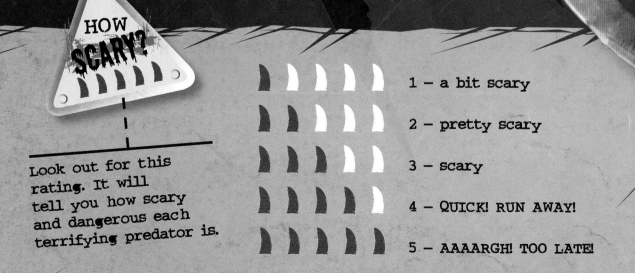

HOW SCARY?

Look out for this rating. It will tell you how scary and dangerous each terrifying predator is.

1 – a bit scary

2 – pretty scary

3 – scary

4 – QUICK! RUN AWAY!

5 – AAAARGH! TOO LATE!

CONTENTS

LION 4

SECRETARY BIRD 6

VAMPIRE BAT 8

CHIMPANZEE 10

WOLVERINE 12

ELECTRIC EEL 14

TIGER 16

TIGER 18

TASMANIAN DEVIL 20

KILLER WHALE 22

WOLF 24

PIRANHA 26

HONEY BADGER 28

POLAR BEAR 30

GLOSSARY 32

TAKING IT FURTHER 33

INDEX 34

Actual size!

Check out this vampire bat on page 8

LION

Lions are unusual big cats. Like most **predators**, they have deadly weapons to catch and kill their **prey**. Unlike most predators, lions hunt in groups.

Even friendly, **tame** lions can suddenly turn on a human and decide it's time to eat!

Lions are strong and smart. They have superb senses of sight and smell, which help them to find antelope and zebras. They live and hunt in family groups called prides.

PREDATOR BITES

Length: Up to 250 cm long

Habitat: African grasslands

Where: Central and southern Africa

Weapons: Massive teeth and claws

HOW SCARY?

KILLER FACT
Lion hunts are most successful on moonless nights. In the dark, prey animals can't see the lions **stalking** them.

4

Lionesses do most of the hunting. They stalk their prey, creeping up close until it is time for the kill. They share the meat with the pride. An adult male can eat up to 43 kg in one go – the weight of a 13-year-old child!

Canine tooth

Actual size!

5 cm

Reasons to kill

Hunting for food is hard work, but it's worth the effort. Meat is packed with energy, so a predator only needs to eat occasionally. By contrast, animals that eat plants need to spend most of their time feeding to get enough energy to live.

SECRETARY BIRD

Raptors have curved bills, which they use to tear the flesh of their prey.

Birds of prey – raptors – are masters of the sky. Most of them have sharp **talons**, hooked bills and huge wings that allow them to swoop through the skies looking for prey.

KILLER FACT

Secretary birds flap their wings when they attack a snake to draw its attention away from the bird's face.

Secretary birds have long legs that allow them to run at high speed.

HOW SCARY?

Secretary birds take to the air during **courtship** as they look for a mate.

Secretary birds are raptors with a difference because they rely on legs, not wings to get around. Although they can fly, these birds spend most of their time on the ground. They walk through long grass searching for grasshoppers, frogs, lizards, tortoises and even venomous snakes.

When the bird senses another animal, it stamps its feet to flush its prey out of the grass. As the animal tries to escape, the secretary bird chases it, stamping it to death with its large feet.

7

VAMPIRE BAT

There are few predators with a worse reputation than the little vampire bat. That's no wonder given their ugly faces, nasty "fangs" and a feeding habit of drinking blood.

Vampire bats sense warm bodies with their noses.

PREDATOR BITES

Length: Up to 95 mm long

Habitat: Forests, grasslands and deserts

Where: Central and South America

Weapons: Sharp little teeth

HOW SCARY?

Vampire bats can run at speeds of up to 8 kilometres per hour.

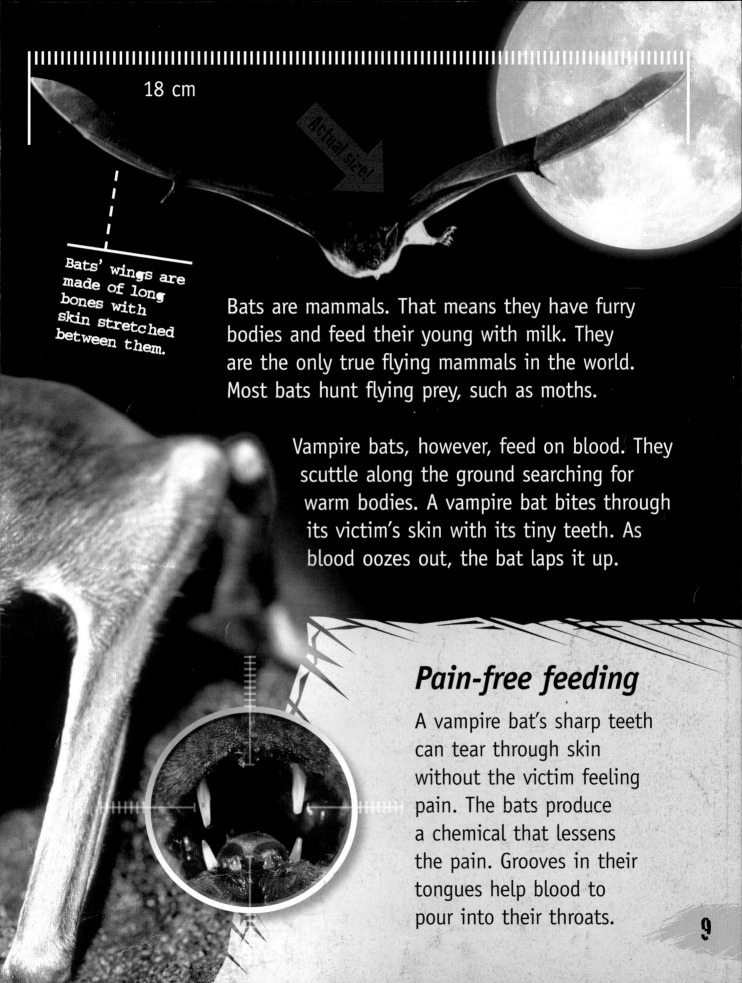

18 cm

Actual size!

Bats' wings are made of long bones with skin stretched between them.

Bats are mammals. That means they have furry bodies and feed their young with milk. They are the only true flying mammals in the world. Most bats hunt flying prey, such as moths.

Vampire bats, however, feed on blood. They scuttle along the ground searching for warm bodies. A vampire bat bites through its victim's skin with its tiny teeth. As blood oozes out, the bat laps it up.

Pain-free feeding

A vampire bat's sharp teeth can tear through skin without the victim feeling pain. The bats produce a chemical that lessens the pain. Grooves in their tongues help blood to pour into their throats.

CHIMPANZEE

Some animal experts think chimpanzees are among the most impressive of all predators. They are fast and clever, and work in a gang to track and kill other animals.

When they feel threatened, chimps bare their teeth.

Tool-makers

Like humans, chimps make tools to use in a hunt. They strip bark from a branch, sharpen it and use it to kill small animals. They also use twigs to dig into termite nests.

KILLER FACT
Chimpanzees are our closest living relatives and some of the cleverest animals alive.

For a long time, scientists thought chimps enjoyed a diet of fruits, leaves, nuts, roots and bugs. Then it was discovered they also prey on pigs and monkeys, and even kill chimps from other families.

These apes hunt cooperatively, which means they work together and have different jobs to do. One chimp might chase a monkey through the trees, while another blocks its escape route and a third waits to **ambush** it.

HOW SCARY?

PREDATOR BITES

Length: Up to 90 cm tall

Habitat: Tropical rainforest

Where: Central Africa

Weapons: Hands and teeth

11

WOLVERINE

These weasel-like animals are no bigger than a dog, but they are brave and fierce enough to attack a bear.

Wolverines live in the world's cold north, where food is scarce. They have long thick fur to keep them warm.

These fearless predators are always on the move, and chase animals much bigger than themselves, such as deer. They leap boldly at their prey, grabbing them in their strong jaws.

Wolverines can kill prey that are many times bigger than them.

A wolverine's jaws are as powerful as those of a crocodile. They can crunch through the large bones of caribou and deer.

KILLER FACT

Wolverines are not just predators. They also scavenge, which means they eat dead animals they find.

PREDATOR BITES

HOW SCARY?

Length: Up to 100 cm

Habitat: Forests and mountains

Where: Northerly regions

Weapons: Massive jaws and crunching teeth

Broad, furry paws help wolverines walk on icy surfaces.

ELECTRIC EEL

Not all predators rely on jaws and claws to catch their prey. Electric eels are fish that **stun** and kill their prey in the most shocking way!

These fish live in the dark, murky waters of the Amazon River, where finding food is a challenge. Electric eels don't have good eyesight. Instead, they use weak electric pulses to find their way, like a **radar** system.

An electric eel also has electric organs along the length of its body. These are used to produce sudden electric shocks that stun the eel's prey or any predators that come too close.

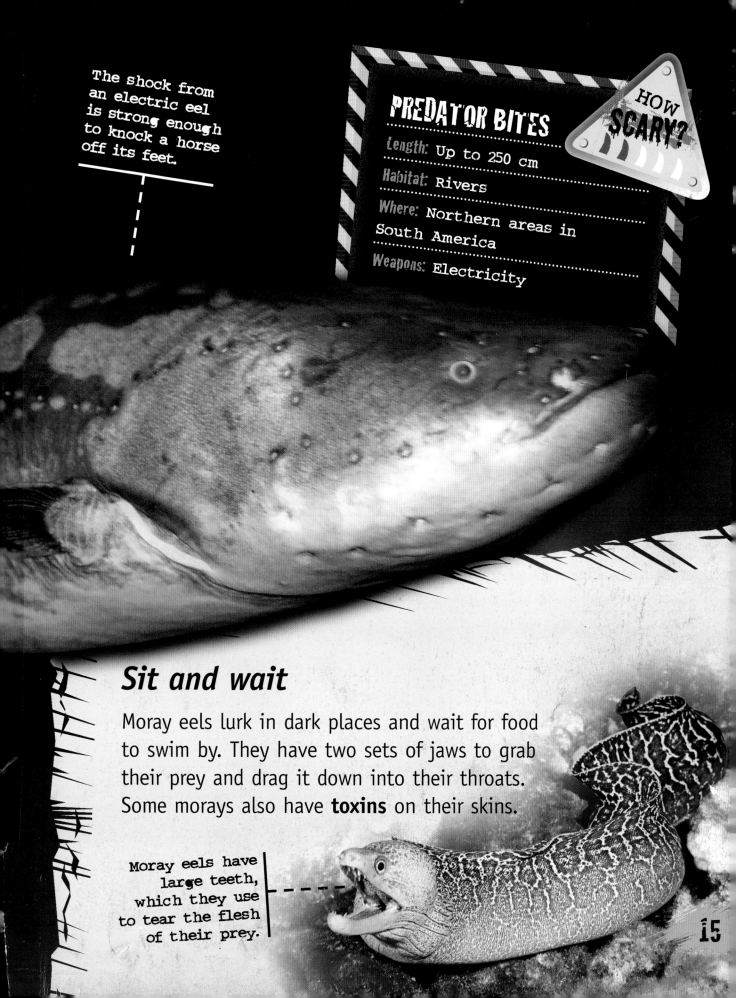

The shock from an electric eel is strong enough to knock a horse off its feet.

PREDATOR BITES

Length: Up to 250 cm

Habitat: Rivers

Where: Northern areas in South America

Weapons: Electricity

HOW **SCARY?**

Sit and wait

Moray eels lurk in dark places and wait for food to swim by. They have two sets of jaws to grab their prey and drag it down into their throats. Some morays also have **toxins** on their skins.

Moray eels have large teeth, which they use to tear the flesh of their prey.

TIGER

Tigers are the largest of all the big cats, and one of the largest of all predators. These majestic animals combine beauty, **stealth** and speed with a deadly instinct to kill.

A tiger's stripes **camouflage** it, keeping it hidden from its prey.

Most tigers live and hunt alone. They patrol their areas, which are called territories, looking for clues that other tigers or other animals are nearby. Tigers have a great sense of smell, which helps them to find prey hiding in the jungle.

PREDATOR BITES

HOW SCARY?

Length: Up to 280 cm

Habitat: Forests, mountains and jungles

Where: Southeast Asia

Weapons: Teeth and claws

TASMANIAN DEVIL

Tasmanian devils deserve their name – they are ferocious and extremely bad-tempered. Devils are famous for their blood-curdling night-time screeches!

Flexible front feet allow devils to hold their food.

Food fight

Tasmanian devils have a great sense of smell. If one devil is feeding, others detect the smell and rush over to share in the feast. Fights sometimes break out over food, but usually the hungry animals just growl at one another.

Devils can eat nearly half their own body weight in just 30 minutes.

Tasmanian devils look like small bears, but they are **marsupials** – a type of mammal that gives birth to tiny young that grow inside a pouch.

These predators survive on a diet of meat, which they get by killing animals, such as wallabies and possums, or by scavenging.

PREDATOR BITES

Length: Up to 80 cm

Habitat: Bush and scrubland

Where: Tasmania

Weapons: Sharp teeth

HOW SCARY?

KILLER WHALE

There is one predator that even a great white shark fears – the killer whale, or orca. These marine mammals are easy to spot, with their striking black and white markings.

Teamwork

Killer whales often live and travel in groups, called pods. They work as a team to catch their prey. Some pods just eat fish, while others prefer to hunt seals or other whales.

Killer whales are very daring in their hunting. Some even risk **beaching** themselves to snatch seals from the shoreline.

A killer whale tries to grab a sea lion from the beach. The whale must be very careful not to get stuck.

Killer whales are successful hunters because they have a range of hunting strategies and prey on many types of animal. Dolphins, whales, sharks, turtles, seals and fish all have good reason to be afraid of killer whales!

HOW SCARY?

PREDATOR BITES

Length: Up to 9 metres

Habitat: Ocean

Where: Worldwide

Weapons: Tail, head and teeth

WOLF

Wolves often appear in fairy tales and legends as cunning killers. They are certainly smart predators with a nose for danger.

During the winter, wolves grow thick, fluffy fur.

PREDATOR BITES

HOW SCARY?

Length: Up to 150 cm

Habitat: Cool forests and mountains

Where: Northerly places

Weapons: Sharp teeth and powerful jaws

The alpha female is the only female in the pack that gives birth to cubs.

Rare beasts

Wolves once roamed large parts of the world, but they are now mostly found in northern forests. They live in groups, called packs, that are ruled by a top male and female called the **alpha pair**.

24

When prey is nearby, wolves give chase, and can run for hours. They work as a team, and may split up to confuse their prey and attack from all sides.

Powerful jaws can crush bones.

KiLLER FaCT
Grey wolves are the largest members of the dog family, and all of our pet dogs are descended from wolves.

Wolves keep in contact with each other over long distances by howling.

Like all dogs, wolves have an incredible sense of smell, and can detect prey, such as rabbits, by their smell more than 2 km away. They can also hear sounds that are 10 km away.

PIRANHA

It is said that a group of piranhas can strip the body of a cow to the bones in minutes. The truth is nowhere near as frightening! These fish can live in large groups, called shoals, but they mostly feed on bugs, small fish and shrimps.

Piranha teeth are pointed and razor-sharp.

Actual size!

PREDATOR BITES

Length: Up to 33 cm long

Habitat: Rivers

Where: South America

Weapons: Sharp teeth

HOW SCARY?

Slice and slash

Piranhas are able to devour flesh easily because their strong jaws are lined with large, triangular teeth that interlock perfectly to make a cutting machine that can slash and slice.

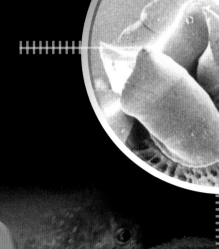

KILLER FACT

People who have been bitten by piranhas have had entire fingers or toes cleanly sliced off!

Piranhas feed at dawn and dusk, when there is little sunlight and they can hide behind water-plants, often in groups of up to 30 fish. Most piranhas attack prey alone.

Occasionally, a number of shoals may gather together into a much larger group to attack and feast on a large animal. However, this is very rare and probably only happens when there is a shortage of food.

27

HONEY BADGER

Honey badgers may have a sweet-sounding name, but they are totally fearless predators. These beasts are programmed to strike and kill, and they are not fussy about what they attack.

KILLER FACT
Honey badgers can kill small crocodiles and pythons that are more than 3 m long!

Badgers live alone and only come together once a year to breed.

These predators explore every avenue in pursuit of food. They dig holes in the ground, searching for worms and bugs, climb trees to raid honey and grubs from bees' nests, and even scamper to upper branches to steal eggs from raptor nests!

HOW
SCARY?

It takes courage to face a lion devouring its prey, head on, and scare that lion away. But that's what honey badgers are prepared to do when they have their sights set on lunch.

Thick skin around the neck and small ears protect the honey badger from injury in fights.

Best friends

Honeyguide birds perch near to bees' nests, and show honey badgers where to dig or climb. Once the badger has opened a nest, the bird swoops in to feast on bees and beeswax.

POLAR BEAR

KILLER FACT
A polar bear needs to kill up to 75 seals every year to survive.

Brown bears and polar bears are the world's largest land meat-eaters. Brown bears have a fearsome reputation, but they do not match polar bears' ruthless approach to hunting.

Polar bears eat most in the winter months, when they can hunt on the sea ice.

PREDATOR BITES

Length: Up to 340 cm

Habitat: The ocean and icy regions

Where: Arctic and Northern Canada

Weapons: Sharp teeth and claws

HOW SCARY?

Polar bears are ferocious hunters and they rely almost entirely on a diet of meat from whales, dolphins and seals. There are few plants in the Arctic so, unlike other bears, they cannot feed on berries or fruits.

Polar bears can survive for up to eight months without food. They are great swimmers, and can run as fast as a human for short stretches. A bear may walk as far as 5,000 km in just one year.

Actual size!

Up to 30 cm

Seal meal

To catch their favourite meal of seal, polar bears must wait by an ice-hole, where seals pop up to breathe. A quick swipe with its massive claws, and a snap of the jaws is all it takes to catch lunch.

Huge feet help bears to walk on snow and to swim quickly.

GLOSSARY

alpha pair
A male and female pair that are the dominant animals in a group such as a pack of wolves.

ambush
To launch a surprise attack from a hidden position.

beaching
When a sea animal, such as a whale, becomes stranded on land.

camouflage
A pattern on an animal's body that hides it from prey or predators.

courtship
A series of rituals, such as flying displays, that animals perform to select a mate.

gorge
To eat a huge amount of food in one go.

marsupial
A kind of mammal, such as a kangaroo or a Tasmanian devil, that gives birth to very small young, which grow in a protective pouch in their mother's body.

predators
Animals that hunt other animals to eat.

prey
Animals that are hunted by predators.

radar
A system that uses radio waves to detect objects. The system gives off radio waves, then senses any waves that bounce back off objects in their way.

stalking
A method of hunting in which a predator follows its prey very quietly. When it gets up close to the prey, it attacks.

stealth
The ability to move very quietly, which allows predators such as tigers to sneak up on their prey.

stun
To knock an animal out suddenly.

talons
The sharp claws of birds of prey.

tame
Not afraid of friendly humans.

toxins
Poisons made by some animals or plants to attack prey or defend themselves from attack.

TAKING IT FURTHER

What makes a predator 'deadly'? Now it's time for you to decide.

- Choose five deadly features, such as speed, size, strength, teeth and claws.

- Use this book, and the Internet, to award up to five points for each of a predator's scary features. Repeat for as many predators as you want.

- Turn your results into a table, graph or chart. Add up the totals to get 'Predator Points' for each animal.

TOP
5
DEADLY
PREDATOR FACTS!

USEFUL WEBSITES

www.kidsbiology.com
This website has a database of hundreds of animals.

www.bigcats.com
Play games and see amazing photos of big cats.

www.bears.org
Are all bears deadly? You can find out here.

gowild.wwf.org.uk
The World Wildlife Fund looks after animals and their homes.

Some experts believe a male chimp is even more dangerous than a male lion.

Wolves will attack bison, which are more than 10 times larger than them.

A killer whale hits seals with its head or thumps them with its tail.

A polar bear can kill an adult walrus that is more than twice its size.

Wolverines often steal the kills of smaller predators such as foxes.

INDEX

alpha pair 24
ambush 11, 15

bats 8–9
beaching 22
bears 30–31
bees 28, 29
big cats 4–5, 16–19
bills 6
birds of prey 6–7
blood 8, 9
breathing 14
breeding 28
brown bear 30

camouflage 16
chase 12, 25
chimpanzee 10–11, 33
co-operative hunting 11
courtship 7

dogs 25

eels 14–15
electric eel 14–15
extinction 17
eyesight 4, 14

feet 13, 20, 31
fights 21, 29
fish 14–15, 26–27
food 5, 7, 11, 17, 21, 23, 26, 28, 31
food fights 21
fur 9, 12, 24

grey wolf 25
groups 4, 10, 11, 22, 24, 27

hearing 25
heat sensors 8
honey badger 28–29
honeyguide bird 29
howling 25
hunting 4, 5, 11, 19, 22, 25, 31

intelligence 4, 11, 24

jaws 13, 19, 25, 27

killer whale (orca) 22–23, 33

leaping 12, 19, 22
legs 6, 7
lion 4–5, 29

mammals 9, 21
marsupials 21
meat 5, 17, 21, 31
moray eel 15

packs 24
piranha 26–27
plants 5, 31
pods 22
polar bear 30–31, 33
prides 4, 5

radar 14
raptors 6–7

scavengers 13, 21
screeching 20
seals 22, 31, 33
secretary bird 6–7
senses 4, 16, 25
shoals 26, 27
Siberian tiger 17
skin 15, 29
smell 4, 16, 21, 25
snakes 6, 7
speed 6, 8, 10, 16, 19, 22, 31
stalking 4, 5, 19
stamping 7
stealth 16
strength 4
stun 14

talons 6
Tasmanian devil 20–21
teeth 9, 10, 15, 27
territories 16
tiger 16–19
tools 11
toxins 15
tracking 10

vampire bat 8–9

whales 22–23
wings 6, 9
wolf 24–25, 33
wolverine 12–13, 33